A History of Paris

The Pont-Neuf.

Thierry Sarmant
Head Curator, Musée Carnavalet

Translated by Angela Caldwell

A History of Paris

Unless stated otherwise, photographs are by Editions Gisserot.

Éditions Jean-Paul Gisserot
www.editions-gisserot.eu

Paris was created by a river, the Seine, which, with its tributaries the Yonne and Marne, enabled trade between the provinces in the east of France and the countries bordering the North Sea. It was also founded here because of its ideal geographical location – a series of islands that provided easy passage across the Seine in a north/south direction. It was this twofold advantage of defensive location and commercial crossroads that, in the 2nd century B.C, led the Gallic tribe known as the *Parisii* to build an *oppidum* (hill fort) on one of the islands and call it Lutetia. The exact site of the hill fort is not known with any certainty. For many years, it was thought to have stood on the Ile de la Cité; current thinking places it on an island located in the area now occupied by Nanterre. Wherever it was, the small town stood in the heart of one of the most fertile agricultural regions in Europe, a region that had been densely populated and undergone improvement since prehistoric times.

Lutetia was razed to the ground during invasion by Julius Caesar in 52 B.C. but it was quickly rebuilt, becoming a medium-sized town in Roman Gaul when the strategic routes

Paris in the reign of King Philip Augustus (13th century).

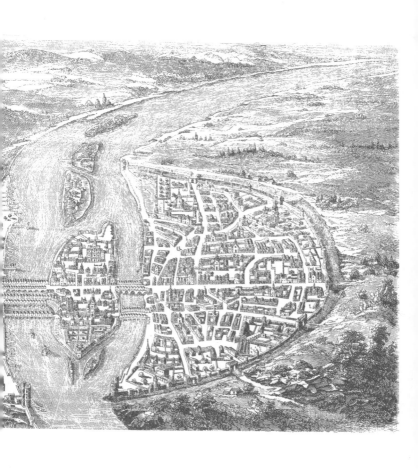

passed further east, starting in Provence and running up to the border, the River Rhine. On the Ile de la Cité stood the governor's palace and a number of temples. The remainder of the town stretched along the left bank, now the Latin Quarter. Only two buildings from the Gallo-Roman town have survived – the Roman arena and the Roman baths in Cluny. The amphitheatre, traditionally referred to as the "Lutetia Arena", was built in the 1st century A.D. on one side of the St. Genevieve Hill so that the natural slope could be put to good use. It could cater for an audience of some 15,000. The Roman baths in Cluny consisted of a vast brick and stone construction, probably built in the early 3rd century A.D. A superb chamber with vaulted roof can still be seen today. Brackets in the shape of the prow of a ship suggest that the construction of the baths may have been sponsored by the corporation of boatmen responsible for the river traffic on the Seine.

One of the few monuments from ancient Lutetia still visible today indicates that the town was something of a melting-pot in which the culture of the defeated Gauls gradually fused with the culture of the victorious Romans. The monument is the Boatmen's Pillar erected during the reign of Emperor Tiberius (14-37 A.D.),

Julius Caesar. Tuileries Gardens.

The Roman baths in Cluny.

The Roman arena.

which was discovered in 1711 beneath the chancel in Notre-Dame. Close by were Celtic gods (Esus, Tarvos Trigarannus, Cernunnos, Smertrios) and Roman divinities such as Jupiter, Vulcan, Mars or Mercury.

Here, as in the remainder of Gaul, the barbarian invasions of the 3rd century destroyed some of the urban area. The Left Bank was abandoned and the stones from its historic buildings used to erect a town wall defending the Ile de la Cité. This was the first such wall in the history of Paris.

In the last centuries of the Empire, Lutetia, a town that had always played a secondary role, began to be called "Paris" i.e. the town of the *Parisii*. In the 4th century, it was large enough to become the seat of a bishopric. During their campaigns in Gaul, two Roman emperors stayed here – Julian in 358 and 360 and Valentinian I in 365 and 366 A.D.

The end of the Roman Empire in the west and the spread of the kingdom of the Franks gave the Paris region a whole new significance. The centre of gravity for the new Merovingian state lay north of the Loire, between the Rhine and the Atlantic. The Mediterranean, once the heart of the Roman world, became an area of division, with different states and cultures, each with its own history. According to chronicler Gregory of Tours, Clovis, the

St. Genevieve by Puvis de Chavannes. The Pantheon.

first Christian king, made Paris the "seat of his kingdom" at the beginning of the 6th century and he was buried there after his death in 511 A.D. During the reigns of his successors, who divided up their territorial inheritance fairly and equally, the town was one of the main seats of power. People returned to the Left Bank. Large abbeys were founded e.g. St. Genevieve's and Sainte-Croix-Saint-Vincent (later Saint-Germain-des-Prés). St. Stephen's Cathedral, built by King Childebert I on the Ile de la Cité, was the largest church in the kingdom of the Franks.

With the arrival of the Carolingian dynasty (751 A.D.), Paris lost its position as the country's prime community. The centre of the Frankish state was the region of Austrasia where the main towns were Aachen, Trier, Mainz, Reims, Laon and Soissons. In the 9th century, Paris was invaded by the Vikings because it lay on a river that was easily navigable. In 885-886 A.D, the town was subjected to a long siege. Its resistance won the day but its suburbs lay in ruins. It is the story of the siege that was told in the first literary work devoted to Paris – a poem in Latin verse written by Abbon the monk under the title, *Bella Parisiacae urbis* (*The Wars of Paris*), and inspired by Virgil's *Aeniad*.

Paris underwent no further expansion for the next hundred years. In 978 A.D, to punish a French raid on

Group sculpture of Charlemagne (1882) in front of Notre-Dame.

Aachen, the German Emperor Otto II laid siege to Paris, setting up camp on the right bank, but he was unable to take the Ile de la Cité. This failed scheme shows that the town was already considered as the main town in the kingdom of France. The same was true when the Capetian dynasty, which owned the county of Paris, finally established itself firmly on the throne (987 A.D). In the 11th century, the Kings of France, whose lands covered no more than the outskirts of Paris and Orleans, ordered the rebuilding of the palace on the Ile de la Cité. The right bank underwent development and became "La Ville" ("The Town"). All that remains of this initial development is one major construction – the westwork at Saint-Germain-des-Prés, built during the abbacy of Father Morard (990-1014) in the Romanesque style.

Paris became the real capital of the kingdom of France in the 12th century, when it was recognised as one of the main centres of intellectual thought in Western Europe. Instruction was initially provided in Notre-Dame's schools and in the abbeys of Saint-Germain-des-Prés, Saint-Victor and Sainte-Geneviève. A poet celebrated this new Jerusalem ("It is near here that David plays the ten-stringed harp") and the number of clerics who studied here was so great that "it almost exceeded the immense multitude of laymen". For his part, Englishman John of Salisbury compared the Paris of scholars to a Jacob's ladder "with its tip touching heaven and angels climbing up and down it".

The University of Paris, which was originally a corporation of masters and students, was set up in the second half of the century. It was given official recognition by King Philip Augustus in 1200 and Pope Innocent III in 1215. From the 13th to 15th centuries, it was the main centre of Catholic theology. The Left Bank, home to the colleges of the University of Paris, was referred to as "the University".

When the State's central institutions became sedentary, Paris seemed a natural choice of location. A decisive step was taken in 1190 when King Philip Augustus set off on a crusade. In an order promulgated that year, the sovereign required that, in his absence, the kingdom's two regents, his mother Queen Adele of Champagne and his uncle Archbishop William the White-Handed, Archbishop of Rheims, should hold audience in Paris every four months. Meanwhile, six burghers of Paris were given responsibility for the royal treasure. In the 13th century, the *Parlement* of Paris and the Exchequer, two major institutions set up by the King's Council, began working in the Palais de la Cité. The first States General met in Paris in 1302 and were again convened there in 1303, 1315, 1317, 1328, 1346 and 1347.

The town's appearance changed. The first major construction site was Notre-Dame, commissioned by Bishop Maurice de Sully (1160-1196) *circa* 1160. Work on the cathedral continued until the 14th century. It displayed a new form of architecture that had first seen the light of day twenty years earlier at the abbey in Saint-Denis; we now refer to it as "Gothic". The building had majestic proportions. It was 125 metres long,

Opposite: the nave of Saint-German-des-Prés.
Overleaf: the nave of Notre-Dame.

The upper chapel in the Sainte-Chapelle, Paris.

12 metres wide in the nave, 41 metres wide on the West Front and 63 metres tall at the towers.

This was followed by the Louvre Palace, a mighty fortress built between 1190 and 1202 to cover the western approaches to the right bank from which the English might continue any offensive launched in Normandy. The circular keep or "large tower" in the Louvre became a symbol of the Capetian dynasty. At the same time, Philip Augustus had a wall build round the Town on the right bank and the University on the Left Bank. Major streets were paved with cobblestones. The large bridge linking the Ile de la Cité to the right bank, and the small bridge linking it to the Left Bank, were rebuilt in stone.

During the reign of St. Louis (1226-1270), luxury buildings continued to be erected. Between 1241 and 1248, the monarch commissioned the building of a masterpiece of Radiating Gothic architecture within the Palais de la Cité. It was the Sainte-Chapelle. In accordance with the tradition of Palatine chapels, the building consisted of a lower chapel (or Lady chapel) on the ground floor for the domestic staff and an upper chapel dedicated to the Holy Crown of Thorns and the Holy Cross, relics of Christ's Passion that St. Louis had obtained from the Latin Emperor of Constantinople, Baldwin II. In the upper chapel, reserved for the royal family and leading into the apartments on the first floor of the palace, the walls were cut away to create a vast reliquary full of multicoloured stained-glass windows.

Circa 1265, the order of Knights Templar, which had had a priory on the right bank since 1139, commissioned the building of a huge square keep flanked by turrets within the so-called "Temple Enclosure". In 1291, after the fall of the last Crusader States in the Holy Land, the Grand Master of the order moved to Paris.

It was also during the reign of St. Louis that the Paris City Council came into being. Initially, there was a "Provost of Merchants" assisted by four aldermen but, by the end of the

La Conciergerie, part of the Law Courts building.

century, there was a "Town Council" made up of the Provost of Merchants, the aldermen and twenty-four town councillors.

In the reign of Philip the Fair (1285-1314), the Capetian monarchy reached the pinnacle of its success. Much of the palace was rebuilt. On the first floor, there was a large chamber with two aisles, decorated with statues of the kings of France. It stood on the site occupied today by the lobby in the Law Courts. The Chamber of the Gentlemen-at-Arms and the Guardroom on the ground floor, both of them roofed with ogival vaulting, still exist. They give some idea of the sheer size of the palace that housed the last members of the direct Capetian line.

The "Chamber of the Gentlemen-at-Arms", Paris Law Courts (14th century).

In 1328, an "Inventory of Parishes and Hearths" in Paris listed 61,098 houses and a population of approximately 200,000. The capital of the kingdom of France was the largest town in the Western world. It dominated the surrounding countryside economically over a distance of 40 to 50 kilometres. The land on the outskirts of the town belonged to Parisian noblemen and crops supplied the capital's markets.

The Hundred Years' War put an end to the prosperity and cast doubt on the role of Paris as the kingdom's nerve centre. The Black Death, which began in 1348, wiped out some of the population. Then the repeated French defeats in the face of attack by the English led to an unprecedented

The Louvre, after *The Very Rich Hours of the Duke of Berry*,
by the Limbourg brothers (15th century).

increase in taxation and tension between the monarch and the Paris Town Council. The Paris Basin (Ile-de-France) was ruined by peasants' revolts, the passage of foreign troops and civil war. In 1419, the English took control of Paris. Henry V of England was quickly recognised as Regent then, upon the death of Charles VI (1422), as King of France. Meanwhile, the deceased king's son, Charles VII, stayed south of the River

Loire. On 16th December 1431, King Henry VI of England was crowned King of France in Notre-Dame. It was not until 1436 that the occupants were put to flight and the legitimate sovereign re-entered Paris.

During the cruel "autumn of the Middle Ages", some respite had been enjoyed in Charles V's reparative reign (1364-1380). A new wall was erected along the right bank and its gate, St. Anthony's Gate, was enlarged and turned into an independent fortress, Bastille Saint-Antoine, soon to be known quite simply as the "Bastille". After riots in 1358, Charles moved from the palace in the City to the Louvre, now located within the town walls, then to the Hôtel Saint-Paul in the Marais District where he commissioned gardens and a menagerie famous for its lions. A vast fortress was built in the east of the town, in Vincennes: its rectangular outer wall was supposed to protect an administrative district that would have been home to the monarch and his main courtiers. To decorate these

The castle keep in Vincennes.

Above and opposite: The Hôtel de Cluny. Now the Museum of the Middle Ages.

buildings, statuary art began to develop. The statues of Charles V and his wife, Joan of Bourbon, which once decorated the entrance of the Célestins church, have survived to the present day. In January 1378, the German Emperor, Charles of Luxembourg and his son, Wenceslas, King of the Romans, came to stay with the King of France. This was the very first official visit to Paris by a foreign Head of State.

The results of the Hundred Years' War were disastrous. By the end of the war, the town had lost half its population – it was home to only 100,000 people in 1436. The major public and private building projects had almost disappeared. During the difficult years at the beginning of his reign, Charles VII had become accus-

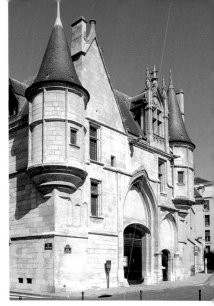

Above: The Hôtel de Sens.

tomed to living in towns and castles in the Loire Valley and his successors followed his example.

After the end of the Hundred Years' War, Paris slowly regained its erstwhile prosperity. It was at this time that the capital's architects opted for the "Flamboyant Gothic" style. Of the private mansions (or "*hôtels*") built at that time, only two have survived – the Hôtel de Sens, the Paris residence of the Archibishops of Sens, ecclesiastical superiors of the Bishops of Paris on the right bank (now the Forney Library), and the Hôtel de Cluny which belonged to the Abbots of Cluny, in the Latin Quarter (now the National Museum of the Middle Ages, *Musée national du Moyen Age*). This residence, a small U-shaped manor house, marked the start of a long line of aristocratic residences built with courtyard on one side and garden on the other, a trend that was to continue until the early 20th century.

In Paris churches, Flamboyant Gothic architecture has also left us some fine buildings e.g. the porch on Saint-Germain-l'Auxerrois, the parish church of the Louvre, the ambulatory in Saint-Séverin on the Left Bank, the belltower on Saint-Jacques-de-la Boucherie and "St. James' Tower" (*Tour Saint-Jacques*) built from 1508 to 1522 near City Hall.

The St. James Tower.

A new Rome
1515-1715.

The monarchy's return to Ile-de-France followed the captivity of King Francis I in Spain (1525-1526). In a letter addressed to the Bureau of the City of Paris dated 15th March 1528, the monarch undertook to "henceforth reside and live most often in his good town and city of Paris and its outskirts rather than in any other place in his kingdom". True to his word, Francis had new residences built and modernised other old royal castles around Paris. Fontainebleau and Saint-Germain-en-Laye were rebuilt; three hunting lodges (Challuau, La Muette and Madrid in the Bois de Boulogne) were brand new constructions. In Paris itself, on the right bank, the King commissioned the laying of the foundation stone of a grandiose church in 1532. Its layout and elevations were inspired by Notre-Dame and it was dedicated to St. Eustace. It was a combination of Gothic structure and Renaissance decoration. In 1533, work began on the building of a new City Hall under the supervision of an Italian architect, Dominico da Cortone, aka Boccador. One year earlier, bookseller Gilles Corrozet had published the first history of Paris, rather pompously entitled *La Fleur des Antiquités* (The Flower of Ancient Times), *singularities and excellence of the most noble and triumphant town and city of Paris, capital of the kingdom of France.*

At the end of his reign, Francis began to turn the Louvre into a palace inspired by the Italian Renaissance. On the site of one of the wings of the castle commissioned by Philip Augustus and Charles V was a new building designed by Pierre Lescot. The work continued under the last Valois sover-

François I by François Clouet.
Louvre Museum.

The Square Courtyard in the Louvre.
Left: The wing designed by Pierre Lescot.

eigns with the construction of the King's Pavilion to the south-west. Further west, Queen Catherine de Medici had the Tuileries Palace built by Philibert Delorme followed by Jean Bullant (1564-1572) and there were ideas of linking this new residence to the Louvre. The architects who worked for the Valois dynasty achieved an unusual blend of Italian design and traditional French architecture. This new style soon spread from royal palaces to private housing and one example of this is the Hôtel de Ligneris, an austere building begun in 1548 (now the Carnavalet Museum).

The Wars of Religion caused a second break between the monarchy and its capital. Paris had been a major

centre for the circulation of new ideas – Humanist Étienne Dolet was burned at the stake there in 1546, the first Protestant Consistory was held there in 1555 and the first National Synod met there in 1559. Most of the people remained staunch supporters of the Roman Catholic religion and were only too willing to believe that the authorities showed weakness or indulgence when it came to heresy. The massacre of Protestants on St. Bartholomew's Day, 24th August 1572, was both a trap planned in high places and a riot by ordinary people. In *Les Tragiques*, poet Agrippa d'Aubigné described the amazing scenes of slaughter, *"with crows blackening the pavilions of the Louvre"*.

From 1588 to 1594, Paris rebelled against its king who was seen as too willing to compose with the Protestants. On 12th May 1588, King Henry III had to flee before rioters in Paris. He was the last of the Valois kings and he was murdered the following year in Saint-Cloud as he prepared to laid siege to the city. In 1590, his cousin and successor, Henry IV, a member of the Protestant religion, failed in a further attempt to reconquer the city. In the following year, a Spanish garrison entered Paris to support the extremist Catholic dictatorship. Henry did not enter his capital until 1594, after he had abjured the Protestant faith. Hence the famous saying, wrongly attributed to King Henry of France and Navarre, that, *"Paris is worth going to Mass for"*.

Like the Valois monarchs, the first Bourbons shared their time between Paris and their castles in the Ile-de-France area, especially Saint-Germain-en-Laye and Fontainebleau. Between 1595 and 1610, Henry IV commissioned the small gallery and the waterside gallery linking the Louvre to the Tuileries. Between 1615 and 1630, his widow, Marie de Medici, commissioned Salomon de Brosse to build her Luxembourg Palace, in a Tuscan style that was supposed to remind her of the Pitti Palace in Florence. Louis XIII continued the work and it led to the creation of the Square Courtyard in the Louvre that we can still see today. For his part, Cardinal de Richelieu, principal minister from 1624, turned an existing mansion into the "Palais-Cardinal" (now known as Palais-Royal) and commissioned architect Jacques Lemercier to build the Church in the Sorbonne (1635-1642) where he had been Rector since 1622.

Since the beginning of the century, other churches, most of them attached to abbeys, were completed or built using designs developed in the Italy of the Counter-Reformation, beginning with the *Gesù* Church in

Portrait of King Henry IV at the Henri IV high school in Paris (kindly authorised by the Head Teacher).

The Luxembourg Palace (Paris) built for Marie de Medici and now the seat of the French Senate.

Rome. Examples can be seen in the West Front of Saint-Gervais, designed by Salomon de Brosse (1615-1621), the Eglise de l'Oratoire by Jacques Lemercier (1622-1745), Saint-Louis, the church of the Jesuits' professed house by Étienne Martellange and François Derand (1627-1641), the church in the Convent of the Daughters of the Visitation designed by François Mansart (1632-1634), the church in the Abbey of Port-Royal by Antoine Le Pautre (1646-1648) and the abbey and church of Val-de-Grâce by François Mansart, Jacques Lemercier and Pierre Le Muet (1645-1662).

The Medici Fountain in the Luxembourg Gardens.

The Sorbonne Church.

Saint-Gervais-Saint-Protais.

Saint-Paul-Saint-Louis.

The church in the Val de Grâce.

These historic buildings embellished the city but did not change its structure. There was little urban planning. The first major project was the construction of the Pont-Neuf at the tip of the Ile de la Cité, the first bridge in Paris to be built without houses on it. Started in 1578, during Henry III's reign, the work was halted during the civil war and was not relaunched until 1600. It was completed in 1607. The next project was Place Dauphine between the Pont-Neuf and the Law Courts (1607-1610). Then Henry IV commissioned the building of Place Royal, now known as Place des Vosges, where the brick and stone houses were built around a rectangular es-

Pont-Royal and the riverside gallery.

planade. An even larger project for a "Place de France" to the north of the Marais district was halted by a lack of investors.

The population of the day was nevertheless impressed by the consistency between the construction of new public buildings, the work commissioned by magistrates and the dynamism of private constructions. Under Henry IV and Louis XIII, Paris was dotted with private mansions belonging to old aristocratic families and magistrates. The Hôtel d'An-goulême, later renamed Hôtel de Lamoignon (now the City Council's Historical Library), was the residence of Diane de France in the Marais district. Work began in 1585, was interrupted by civil war and completed in 1611-1612. The Hôtel de Sully in Rue Saint-Antoine was built to designs by Jean Androuet du Cerceau between 1625 and 1630. The Ile Saint-Louis, the island formed by the combining of Ile Notre-Dame and Ile aux vaches, was divided into building plots between 1614 and 1656. Between 1639

Place des Vosges (Marais District).

and 1644, Louis Le Vau built a sumptuous mansion at the southern tip of the island for President Lambert. It was with reference to these projects that, in his play *Le Menteur* (*The Liar,* 1642), Corneille had the hero, Dorante, who had returned to the capital after a period in the province, declare, "Paris seems to my eyes a land of novels. / I thought this morning to see an enchanted island. / I left it deserted and find it now inhabited. / A new Amphion, without the help of stone-

Hôtel de Lamoignon (Marais District).

Hôtel de Sully (Marais District).

Hôtel Lambert (Ile Saint-Louis).

masons, / Has changed these bushes into superb palaces... / [...] An entire town, built with pomp, / Seems to have risen by miracle from an old ditch, / And has us presume, by its superb roofs, / That all its people are gods or kings".

Another crisis between the monarchy and Paris occurred between 1648 and 1652 – the Fronde Revolt. On two occasions, in 1649 and 1651, the young Louis XIV had to flee the capital. He never forgot it. It broke his trust and, after 1671, the king never again lived in Paris. In 1682, the Court moved to Versailles and, with the exception of a brief period during the Regency (1715-1722), the King of France only made a few fleeting appearances in Paris. It would take nothing less than a revolution to bring the sovereign back to the banks of the Seine.

Louis XIV in his Coronation Robes (1701), by Hyacinthe Rigaud. Louvre Museum.

Although the monarchy was absent from the city, it nevertheless covered the capital with public buildings designed to turn Paris into a "new Rome". In the reign of Louis XIV, the old walls were demolished to leave

Perrault's colonnade. Louvre Museum.

Collège des Quatre-Nations, now the Institute of France.

room for a "new boulevard" on the right bank. The same period saw the building of the Louvre Colonnade (Claude Perrault, 1667-1670), the Observatory (Perrault, 1667), the gates in Saint-Denis (Blondel, 1672) and Saint-Martin (Pierre Bullet, 1674), the Hôtel royal des Invalides

Louis XIV's Visit to the Hôtel royal des Invalides, on 14th July 1701 (detail)
by Pierre-Denis Martin. Carnavalet Museum.

(Libéral Bruand and Jules Hardouin-Mansart, 1671-1678), Place des Victoires (Hardouin-Mansart, 1685-1692), Place Louis-le-Grand and Place Vendôme (Hardouin-Mansart, 1685-1703). All these buildings were full of references to both the Ancient Romans and the Rome of the Baroque period with its columns, colossal pilasters and domes. And all these buildings were erected to the glory of the Sun King. A relief of the monarch can be seen above the entrance to Les Invalides, a full-length statue stands in the middle of Place des Victoires and there is an equestrian statue in the centre of Place Vendôme. The masterpiece of this Classical architecture is the dome on Les Invalides, built by Hardouin-Mansart who sought inspiration in the designs and drawings left by his great-uncle, François Mansart. And it was to see this dome that Louis XIV came to Paris for the last time, on 28th August 1706.

The dome on the Invalides.

The City of Enlightenment
1715-1789

The absence of the sovereign did not change Paris' role as the nation's capital. In his memoir, *L'importance dont Paris est à la France* (The Importance of Paris to France) written in the 1680s, Vauban described the town as the "true heart of the kingdom, the mother of the French people and a summary of France, through which all the peoples in this great State live and without which the kingdom could not survive without a considerable decline in its grandeur". After learning about urban planning from towns in Italy, Paris became a model in its turn, for France as a whole. "Royal squares" copying those in the capital were built in the provinces in the reigns of Louis XIV and Louis XV. Ministers kept on their private mansions in Paris and travelled from Versailles to do business there. The Parliament of Paris still functioned in the city. Paris was the kingdom's financial and economic centre, and the intellectual heart of Europe. Its fashions spread right across the continent. Its Academies and *salons* welcomed intellectual monsters from every country. "Paris is a huge farmyard filled with strutting turkey cocks

The Boatmen's Joust at Notre-Dame Bridge by Nicolas Raguenet (1756). Carnavalet Museum.

The Hôtel de Soubise, now the National Archives (Marais District).

and parrots repeating words without hearing them", railed Voltaire in 1776. Foreigners flocked to Paris. For the first time since 16th century, the city received visits from reigning monarchs – Tsar Peter the Great in 1717, Gustave III of Sweden in 1771 and Emperor Joseph II in 1777. And Paris retained its rebellious spirit, convinced as it was of its superiority over the royal place of residence. "I hate Versailles", wrote Montesquieu, "because everybody is small there. I love Paris because, here, everybody is great". There was a touch of bitterness in his disdain: "The capital would be superb and rich", noted Louis-Sébastien Mercier in his *Tableau de Paris*, "if Louis XIV, instead of building Versailles for himself, had built Paris for his people".

The building of huge private mansions continued throughout the Sun King's reign, even after the wars and financial crises had put an end to official building projects. In fact, the enthusiasm for construction continued throughout the 18th century. The most opulent of the houses in the Marais district, the Hôtel de Soubise, was built to plans by Pierre-Alexis Delamair from 1704 onwards, during the War of the Spanish Succession. In 1705, the same architect oversaw the foundation work for the Hôtel de Rohan, the last magnificent mansion to be built in the Marais district. The beginning of Louis XV's reign brought with it the Hôtel d'Évreux, now the Élysée Palace (Claude-Armand Mollet, 1718-1720), the Hôtel de Matignon

Place de la Concorde.

(Jean Courtonne, 1722-1724), the Bourbon Palace and the Hôtel de Lassay (Jean Aubert, 1727-1730) and the Hôtel de Biron, now the Rodin Musem (Jean Aubert). The outline of the mansions changed. In place of the U-shape favoured until 1660 came a more compact layout that was easier to integrate into the long, narrow plots of land. The houses were lower, sometimes consisting of no more than a ground floor and flat roof, like the Grand Trianon in Versailles (Bourbon Palace).

The military academy.

St. Genevieve's Church, now the Pantheon.

The Mint, Quai de Conti.

In the 1750s, after several decades of inactivity, major public building projects were restarted and there was a determination to equal the legacy of the century in which Louis XIV reigned. Place Louis XV (now Place de la Concorde, 1766-1775) was designed by Ange-Jacques Gabriel, the king's leading architect. It provided the backdrop for an equestrian statue of the sovereign by Bouchardon that was inaugurated in 1763. The frontages overlooking the square were inspired by the colonnade on the Louvre. The Military Academy, built on the Grenelle Plain to plans by Gabriel, was intended to offset the Invalides commissioned by the Sun King (1761-

1773). St. Genevieve's Church (now the Pantheon) was designed by Jacques-Germain Soufflot from 1757 and completed during Louis XVI's reign. It is reminiscent not only of the Invalides, but also of St. Peter's Basilica in Rome and St. Paul's Cathedral in London.

Over the last few years of pre-Revolutionary France, there was a fashion for majestic buildings to house institutions that, until then, had been content with more modest accommodation. One example of this is the Hôtel des Monnaies (the Mint, 1767-1775) designed by Jacques-Denis Antoine, a veritable palace-cum-factory on the banks of the Seine that highlighted the prosperity of the kingdom of France. In the reign of Louis XVI, Jacques Gondoin built the College of Surgery (1776-1786), an example of architecture inspired by the Ancient Greeks and Romans, while Marie-Joseph Peyre and Charles de Wailly built the "French Theatre" (now the Odeon, 1779-1783) near the Luxembourg Palace, showing the obvious influence of Palladio.

"Neoclassical" architecture also became popular for private dwellings including the Hôtel du Châtelet built by Mathurin Cherpitel between 1770 and 1776, the Hôtel de Bourbon-Condé built by Brongniart in 1780-1782, or the Hôtel de Salm (now the Palace of the Legion of Honour) built by Pierre Rousseau between 1782 and 1787. The same fashion spread to religious architecture where inspiration was found in paleo-Christian basilicas. The most famous example of this trend is the Church of Saint-Philippe-du-Roule, built by Chalgrin between 1774 and 1784.

Paris continued to expand. It had a population of 400,000 in 1637 and more than 600,000 in 1789. With such continual expansion, the city outgrown its old boundaries. It had also moved westwards. At the end of the reign of Louis XIV, the suburb of Saint-Germain replaced the Marais as the fashionable place to live. "It is here", wrote somebody in 1763, "that the kingdom's leading nobility live and there are therefore very many magnificent mansions here". In Louis XV's reign, development in the north-west gave rise to the suburb of Saint-Honoré, the Chaussée d'Antin, and the suburbs of Poissonnière, Montmartre Saint-Denis and Le Temple. In the second half of the century, a new type of building appeared – investment property (Odeon district). But while the old mediaeval centre within Charles V's walls was very densely developed with narrow houses four, five or six storeys high, the private residences in the suburbs stood next to one or two-storey houses and there was a great deal of open land as well as workshops, sheds, vegetable plots and flower gardens.

From 1784 to 1787, a new town wall with no defensive purpose was erected around Paris, which had been an open town since the 1670s. This was the "Farmers' General Wall" 23 kilometres long, designed to make it easier to obtain taxes on goods at the town's tollgates. Architect Claude-Nicolas Ledoux was commissioned to build "toll booths" and he favoured an austere, powerful neo-Palladian style. The Parisians, however, remained unmoved by these refinements and a famous saying of the time ("Le mur murant Paris rend Paris murmurant") states that the wall around Paris led to grumblings among the general public.

The Rotunda in La Villette.

People at that time were especially aware of the gap between the prestige of the capital and the often unappealing appearance of its outskirts. In his *Confessions*, Jean-Jacques Rousseau described his disappointment upon arriving in Paris in 1731, "I had imagined a town as beautiful as it was large, impressive in appearance, with nothing but superb streets and palaces of gold and marble. I arrived through the suburb of Saint-Marceau and saw only small, dirty, stinking streets and ugly black houses, steeped in a general air of filth and poverty, with beggars, carters, garment menders and vendors of herbal infusions and old hats".

Theorists and architects began to dream of an ideal Paris with sumptuous monuments, straight roads and orderly facades. In short, a clean, rational, organised city. In 1770, in a work of imagination entitled *L'An 2440, rêve s'il en fut jamais* (The year 2440, a dream if there ever was), Louis-Sébastien Mercier allowed himself to imagine the city of the future, "Roofs of equal height formed a vast garden and the city, seen from the top of a tower, was crowned with flowers, fruit and greenery".

A time of revolution
1789-1914

The French Revolution did not begin in Paris but it very quickly moved to the city. Politically speaking, everything was played out in Versailles on 17th June 1789 when the States General, opened by Louis XVI on 5th May, declared themselves to be a National Assembly. The riots in Paris merely emphasised the weakening of royal authority. On 14th July, the Bastille was taken. Little matter that the fortress was almost unused and that the resistance had been insignificant, it was the symbol of absolute monarchy, of the centuries-old surveillance of the capital by Power – and it fell. The destruction of the building began almost immediately. On 17th July, Louis XVI travelled to Paris, donned the three-coloured cockade and recognised the National Guard, an offshoot of the bourgeois militia, and the Commune that had replaced the legal authorities. On 6th October, the King was forcibly brought from Versailles to Paris. He moved into the Tuileries Palace.

The Bastille in the First Days of its Destruction by Hubert Robert. Carnavalet Museum.

The Festival of the Federation (detail) by Charles Thévenin. Carnavalet Museum.

From then on, the drama of the Revolution was played out in Paris. The Festival of the Federation, which marked the reconciliation of the French people, was held there on 14th July 1790. The Legislative Assembly created by the new Constitution sat for the first time in the riding ring at the Tuileries on 1st October 1791. On 10th August 1792, it was a riot in Paris that brought about the fall of the monarchy. It was in Paris, on the following 5th September, that the provisional executive committee proclaimed "Terror to be the order of the day". It was in Paris, on Place Louis XV renamed Place de la Révolution, that Louis XVI and Marie-Antoinette mounted the scaffold, on 21st January and 16th October 1793. " Paris is not like other towns; it does not belong to its people", wrote Camille Desmoulins. "Paris is the common country, the mother country of all French people". For almost one hundred years, France followed in the footsteps of the capital.

Members of the old hereditary aristocracy and wealth-based elite emigrated or went to the guillotine in their thousands. The assets belonging to clergy or émigrés became "national property" until such time as it was sold off. There was a vast redistribution of wealth, which benefitted both the State and the elite created by the Revolution. In the 19th and 20th centuries, many government bodies and public authorities occupied former convents, abbeys or private residences.

The Coronation of Napoleon (detail) by Jacques-Louis David. Louvre Museum.

The regimes that followed each other after the Reign of Terror rightfully mistrusted Paris. The Directoire took steps to limit municipal independence and, on 13 Vendémiaire of Year IV (5th October 1795) it ordered the last Parisian uprising to be put down by a young General named Napoleon Bonaparte. After becoming First Consul (1799) then Emperor of the French People (1804), Bonaparte took the Tuileries Palace as his official residence and put the city under the control of the Prefect of the Seine, a *de facto* Mayor, and of the Prefect of Police, a title replacing the former Lieutenant General of Police. The Bourbon and Orléans dynasties kept these institutions in place but that did not prevent the Restoration and the July Monarchy from losing power as a result of riots in Paris, in July 1830 and February 1848.

It was during this period of revolution that Paris lost its mediaeval cloak and became the "City of Light" that has survived almost intact into the 21st century. During the Revolution, a time of economic and financial crisis, people dreamed of grandiose monuments while destroying some of the monuments that symbolised the monarchy. Churches and convents were demolished but there was little new building. The results from the days of the Consulate and Empire are much more significant. The major projects designed in the days of the monarchy were taken up again and new constructions inspired by the Ancient Romans or Greeks saw the light of day. They included Rue de Rivoli on which work started in 1801, the facade of the Legislative Body (now the National Assembly, 1804-1807), the Arc de triomphe du Carrousel (1806), the Arc de triomphe on Place de l'Étoile (1806, completed in 1833), the church dedicated to Mary Magdalen (La Madeleine, begun in 1807, completed in 1842) and the Stock Exchange (1813). The first land register in Paris came into being between 1806 and 1821.

The Church of St. Mary Magdalen.

Even bigger projects such as a palace for the King of Rome, which would have been built on Chaillot Hill, were either abandoned shortly after they began or remained on the

The Arc de Triomphe.

The Carrousel triumphal arch.

drawing board. There were ideas about totally transforming the city by creating new roads and dividing entire districts into plots of building land. "I had dreams", wrote Napoleon in his *Mémorial de Sainte-Hélène*, "of making Paris the real capital of Europe. Sometimes, I wanted it to become a city with a population of 2, 3 or 4 million, something fabulous, gigantic, something never before seen, with public buildings that satisfied the population's demands". The fall of his Empire, marked by two consecutive periods of occupation of Paris by allied troops in 1814 and 1815, adjourned these undertakings. It was left to the Second Empire to build the projects of the First, and it did so on a grand scale.

Liberty Guiding the People by Eugène Delacroix. Louvre Museum.

Napoleon's tomb in the Invalides.

The Restoration and July Monarchy had more modest effects on the Paris landscape. Between 1815 and 1830, the Bourbons continued with the building of the Arc de triomphe and commissioned numerous churches in the neo-Classical style e.g. Notre-Dame de Lorette (1823-1836), Saint-Vincent-de-Paul (1834-1844) and Saint-Denis-du-Saint-Sacrement (1826-1835). Louis-Philippe, King of the French People from 1830 to 1848, had a column commemorating the July revolution erected in the middle of Place de la Bastille. Anxious to achieve national reconciliation, he had the Luxor obelisk erected on Place de la Concorde (1836) and commissioned Napoleon's monumental tomb beneath the dome of the Invalides. Influenced by English ideas, vast areas were turned over to residential development in the late 1820s and in the 1840s but progress was halted by the crises that preceded the revolutions in 1830 and 1848. The July Monarchy was responsible for only one piece of

The July Column, Place de la Bastille.

Napoleon III giving Haussmann the Law Annexing Outlying Villages, on 16th June 1859
by Adolphe Yvon. Carnavelet Museum.

town planning – the laying of the future Rue Rambuteau, a street running in an east-west direction along the right bank on which work began in 1838. The main contribution of this monarchy was the construction of the fortified "Thiers" wall between 1841 and 1845. It was designed to defend the "unique centre, the driving force that moves everything. Attack this centre and France is like a man struck on the head", wrote Adolphe Thiers in 1840. In all, the contribution was minor in a city with a population of one million in 1848. To cater for the increased population, the houses were built upwards and plots of land were less widely-spaced. The urban landscape was changed only slightly, but for the worse.

People then began to express an interest in the history and buildings of Paris. In 1821, Dulaure began to publish a very successful *History of Paris*. Then, in 1831, came the publication of *Notre-Dame de Paris*, Victor Hugo's historic novel known to English-speakers as *The Hunchback of Notre-Dame*, in which the cathedral provides the backdrop and is also the main character. Successive generations of Romantics discovered the charms of "Old Paris" and lamented its gradual passing.

When Napoleon III became emperor, Paris still looked much as it had before the Revolution. Between 1853 and 1870, the Emperor and Baron Haussmann, Prefect of Paris, commissioned some decisive changes that gave the town the appearance it has retained until the present day. By a decree signed in 1859, Napoleon III ordered the annexation of the old suburbs to the city. Thus redesigned, it lay more or less within the "Thiers wall". It was redivided into twenty new districts or "*arrondissements*" and, one hundred and fifty years later, they still give structure to Parisian life. Wide, straight boulevards were laid out, running in all directions and destroying entire portions of districts in the city centre. "Old Paris has gone", wrote poet Charles Baudelaire. "Alas, the shape of a town changes more quickly than the heart of a mortal". The new roads were lined with uni-

formly-designed investment properties referred to in later years as "Haussmann-style buildings". They were the distant cousins of the residences built on Hardouin-Mansart's orderly squares and they used polite, formulaic architectural features – basements with bosses, hierarchical upper floors and the use of architectural orders and balconies. Four new bridges and a viaduct spanned the River Seine. Modern amenities were created, including sewers, pavements, a new central market, landscaped parks and railway stations. The first department stores opened their doors, the very first one being Le Bon Marché, founded by Aristide and Marguerite Boucicaut in 1852.

The opera house designed by Garnier.

Supporters of the Commune with the statue of Napoleon after the fall of the Vendôme Column.
Photograph : Montmartre Museum.

The finishing touch during the Second Empire was the commissioning of a number of prestigious buildings. Paris was carpeted with Town Halls and churches in the neo-Romanesque, neo-Gothic and neo-Renaissance styles. The secular Louvre project was completed – the Tuileries Palace was linked to the Louvre and the area surrounding the palace was totally cleared, as directed by Hector Lefuel. The Law Courts and National Library were partly rebuilt. However, the construction that best symbolises the Second Empire remains the opera house designed by Charles Garnier in a sumptuous eclecticism that was an attempt to create a "Napoleon-III" style. In its day, it was the largest opera house in the world (1862-1875).

Imperial prosperity, though, ended in tragedy. On 19th July 1870, France declared war on Prussia. On 2nd September, the French Army surrendered in Sedan and the Emperor was taken prisoner. On 4th September, the Republic was proclaimed in Paris. At the end of the month, Paris was besieged. On 18th January 1871, the German Empire was proclaimed in the Great Gallery in Versailles and, on 1st March, the Prussians entered Paris. On 18th March, a number of

Parisians rebelled against the legal authorities and set up a revolutionary power – the Commune. Instead of being overturned by the riots, as every power base in France had been since 1789, the government moved to Versailles, already the seat of the National Assembly, and started to bring the capital to heel by force. The civil war ended with victory on the part of those in Versailles, a period of savage repression and the destruction of public buildings set on fire by supporters of the Commune in the last few days of the struggle, known as the "Bloody Week" (21st to 28th May 1871). Among the buildings destroyed were the old City Hall, the Tuileries Palace, part of the Law Courts and the Palais-Royal but many other public and private buildings suffered damage at that time.

After the Commune, the cycle of revolution and peace ended. Paris never again imposed its law on France. And despite the triple, traumatic setbacks of siege, defeat and the Commune, the city continued to expand. The population rose from two million in 1877 to almost three million by 1911, a figure that has never again been equalled. The buildings that lay in ruins were slowly rebuilt, with the exception of the Tuileries Palace and the Palais d'Orsay, both of which were eventually demolished. Town planning projects slowed but

The Sacré-Coeur.

private construction continued and the "Haussmann-style buildings" survived the passing of their originator. After 1900, the development of the automobile and the construction of the Underground (the "Métro") changed everyday life and contributed to the development of the suburbs.

Official architecture remained loyal to the concept of eclectism, resulting in public buildings that were

The Palais du Trocadéro designed by Davioud and replaced, in 1937, by the Palais de Chaillot.

often uninteresting. Between 1877 and 1923, a basilica church dedicated to the Sacred Heart was built on the hilltop in Montmartre to designs by Paul Abadie. Built in the "Romanesque-Byzantine" style, the Sacré Coeur and its tall domes draw the eye because of the whiteness of the Château-Landon limestone with which it is clad. The largest public buildings were erected for the world fairs in 1878, 1889 and 1900. Between 1876 and 1878, Gabriel Davioud designed the Palais du Trocadéro,

The Eiffel Tower in 1889. Private collection.

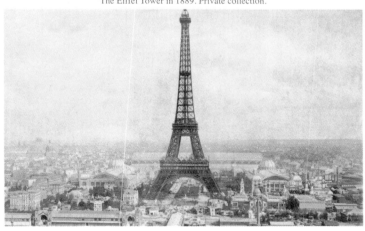

The building of the Paris underground, Place Saint-Michel circa 1905. Carnavalet Museum.

a strange semi-circular building flanked by two tall towers and extended by two curved wings. The best-known legacy of the 1889 exhibition, which commemorated the centenary of the French Revolution, is the metal tower designed by engineer Gustave Eiffel. With a height of 300 metres, it was then the tallest building in the world. It was also one of the most unpopular; it was described as the "dishonour of Paris" and an "odious column of bolted metal". The 1900 exhibition produced some less controversial buildings – the Orsay railway station, the lavishly-decorated Alexander III bridge and the Grand Palais and Petit Palais, one designed to hold exhibitions and the other to serve as the City of Paris art gallery. On the eve of the First World War, although new building materials and construction techniques were available, most of the architects remained faithful to a language that drew its inspiration from the styles of the past.

An aerial view of the Grand Palais.

The First World War put a halt to the expansion of Paris within the limits set for it by Napoleon III. From then on, the number of people living "within the walls" (i.e. in the city centre) continued to drop while the suburbs became more and more densely populated until they covered almost all of the former "county" of Seine and, shortly afterwards, much of Ile-de-France. In the early 21st century, the twenty districts ("*arrondissements*") in Paris have a population of approximately two million, as many as in 1870, and ten to twelve million people (depending on the counting methods) live in suburbs on its doorstep. The city has gone from metropolis to megacity.

Within the 1860 boundaries, the city's structure has undergone little significant change but, towards the end of the Third Republic, Paris nevertheless gained a series of buildings for which the inspiration was powerful and unusual – and they were far superior to the pre-war designs. To mark the Colonial Exhibition in 1931, Albert Laprade built the Colonial Museum (*Musée des Colonies*) at the *Porte Dorée*. The museum pays homage to the French Empire with an 89-metre main façade sculpted along its entire length, forming a "tapestry in

The "Golden Doorway" to the Colonial Museum.

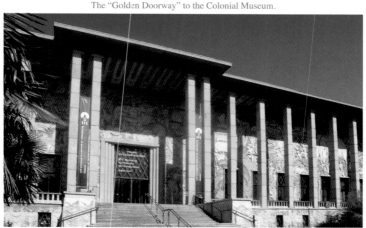

The Palais de Chaillot.

stone" behind a peristyle of slender pillars. For the 1937 World Fair, three large buildings were erected – the Palais de Tokyo, the *Musée des travaux publics* (Museum of Public Works) and the Palais de Chaillot. In the Palais de Tokyo (Aubert, Dondel, Viard and Dastugue), which houses the Modern Art Gallery, there is another peristyle similar to the one already used for the *Musée des Colonies*. At the *Musée des travaux publics*, a masterpiece by Auguste Perret on Place d'Iéna (now housing the Economic and Social Council), a vast rotunda flanked by slender columns contains a conference room. The Palais de Chaillot stands on the site of the former Palais du Trocadéro. In place of a heavy rotunda, Jacques Carlu designed a spectacular vista linking Place du Trocadéro to the Seine. This is the most significant example of the new French Classicism.

In addition to these few buildings in the centre of Paris, the main legacy of the interwar years was the ring of low-cost housing built on the site of the Thiers Wall, which was demolished from 1920 onwards. Often built with a brick facing, the buildings stand out from later projects for the attention to detail and the quality of the construction.

In its embellished state, Paris remained a universal object of admiration and envy. On 23rd June 1940, Adolf Hitler, whose troops had just soundly defeated the French Army, gazed out over the city from the Trocadéro. In the evening, he said to Albert Speer, his favourite architect: "Isn't Paris beautiful? We now have to make sure that Berlin becomes even more beautiful. In the past, I often wondered whether we should not destroy Paris. But by the time we have finished with Berlin, we shall have put Paris completely in the shade. So why bother destroying it?" In fact, neither the First nor the Second World Wars affected the Paris landscape. The air raids of 1918, the German Occupation between 1940 and 1944 and the fighting to liberate the city in August 1944 did not lead to massive destruction. It was a good fortune not enjoyed by other European capitals such as London or Berlin.

Until the post-war era, the architecture of private housing was an ex-

Hitler posing, with the Eiffel Tower in the background.
German troops parading down the Champs-Elysées.
Photos from a German Red Cross book (July 1940). Private collection.

tension of Haussmann-style town planning in terms of design and building traditions. The change came in the 1960s when buildings of glass and

The Défense District.

steel became popular and new town planning regulations allowed property speculation to cast off the restrictions of previous times. Paris emerged from this period much uglier than it had been before, especially in the outer-most *arrondissements*, but the basic layout remained unchanged. The 210-metre Montparnasse Tower, built between 1969 and 1973 next to the railway station of the same name, was a blot on the landscape along much of the Left Bank. On a lesser scale, the tower block on the Jussieu university campus similarly affected the Latin Quarter. Throughout Paris, tower blocks lost all sense of scale, freed from the former constraints of alignment and buildings in rows, totally heedless of their environment.

The main success as regards this new architecture was the Défense district built on land within Puteaux and Courbevoie, extending the line of the Champs-Elysées and forming an end point to the vista. It was decided to build this business district in 1955 and it immediately became a centre for experimental design. In 1957, the *Centre national des industries et techniques* (CNIT, national industry and technology centre) was built there – a vast vaulted roof of concrete on three supports. In the following decades, a landscape of mineral open spaces and towers was created in the Défense district, instilling it with a sort of futuristic majesty.

Roads also underwent change in the face of demand from the automobile. Between 1942 and 1973, a 35-kilometre ring road was built, a veritable urban motorway located more or less on the unbuilt section of the Thiers Wall. This virtual fortification isolated the twenty *arrondissements* of 1860 from the suburbs as completely as the old fortified walls had once separated Paris from its suburbs. The "riverside expressways" cutting the town off from the River Seine, the "red routes" that turn avenues into traffic-packed roads, cut swathes through the urban fabric.

With an eye to posterity, the Presidents of the Fifth Republic again took up the monarchist tradition of grand official buildings. Charles de Gaulle and his Minister of Cultural Affairs, André Malraux, were content to clean up and repair the frontages of the capital's historic buildings but later Presidents were more ambitious. Georges Pompidou (1970-1974) left his name to the strange coloured pipes and tubes of the Centre Pompidou (designed by Renzo Piano and Richard Rogers, 1971). Valéry Giscard d'Es-

The Georges-Pompidou Centre.

The Orsay Museum.

taing (1974-1981) decided to turn the Orsay railway station into a museum of 19th-century art; it was not opened until 1986. François Mitterrand (1981-1995), the Builder-President, inaugurated the Grand Louvre (Ieoh Ming Pei, 1983-1989), the *Institut du monde arabe* (Institute of the Arab World by Jean Nouvel, 1987), the Opéra de la Bastille (the opera house designed by Carlos Ott, 1989), the *Grande Arche de la Défense* (the Great Arch in the Défense District by Johann Otto von Spreckelsen, 1989) and the *Bibliothèque nationale de France* (French national library by Dominique Perrault, 1995). The *leitmotivs* are obvious in Mitterrandian projects – a love of the monumental, a wish for grandeur and a taste for simple geometric forms such as the pyramid, rectangle and semi-circle. Jacques Chirac, President after being Mayor of Paris (1995-2007), gave his name to only one major project, the *Musée des Arts premiers* (Museum of

Primitive Arts) on Quai Branly, designed by Jean Nouvel and opened in 2006.

The aesthetic results of these major projects are, in many cases, controversial. The huge glass and steel constructions are at odds with the dimensions and colours of Haussmann's city. In their determination to mark their incursion into the limited area that is old Paris, symbolically at least, the authorities often got things wrong. In what has become the most popular tourist destination in the world, most of the contemporary buildings have great difficulty trying to blend in. Now, how-

The Louvre Museum.

ever, large-scale projects are no longer possible, or desirable, other than within the wider megacity.

Political and administrative structures are finding it difficult to keep up with galloping urbanisation. In 1968, seven new *départements* ("counties") were created. The *département* of Seine, which included Paris, was divided into four new *départements*: Paris, Hauts-de-Seine, Seine-Saint-Denis and Val-de-Marne, forming what is now known as the "inner ring" around Paris. At the same time, the former *département* of Seine-et-Oise was subdivided into three *départements*: Essonne, Val-d'Oise and Yvelines. With Seine-et-Marne, these *départements* form the "outer ring". In 1977, the city elected its mayor for the first time in history. The victor was Jacques Chirac, who retained the position until 1995. In 1982, the laws on decentralisation gave new powers to the *départements* and regions.

This series of reforms, however, did not put an end to France's domination by Paris. Demographically, economically, culturally and intellectually, it remains the head of the nation and the State, albeit in a hypertrophied form. The regional network of express trains (RER) built between 1962 and 1977 allowed the suburbs to spread in tentacular fashion and the development of the high-speed train (TGV) network is now turning most of the towns within the Paris Basin into suburbs of the capital.

Pulled in different directions by rival authorities (State, Paris City Council, *départements* and Ile-de-France region), the megacity that is Paris is seeking a leader. Never have the political and administrative leaders been so far removed from economic and social reality. The old Paris "within the walls" is now a town-museum in which it would be unthinkable to build anything on a grand scale without damaging an exceptional heritage or compromising the harmony of the urban landscape. As to the suburbs, martyred by half a century of disorderly construction, they are waiting for a grand design, the town planning and public buildings that they so lack. This will be the birthplace of the Paris of the future, the "Great Paris" whose outlines have yet to be invented.

Jacques Chirac, Mayor of Paris from 1977 to 1995. Private collection.

Contents

The author would like to thank the following people for their help and advice :
Jean-Marc Léri, Danielle Chadych, Jean-Philippe Dumas, Alexandre Gady,
Marie-Claire Hubert and Florian Meunier.
The publisher would like to thank the Carnavalet and Montmartre Museums.

©2010 Éditions Gisserot
Imprimé et façonné par Pollina Luçon 85 n° d'impression : L55975
Imprimé en France